The ULTIMATE Guide to

WOMEN'S FOOTBALL

YVONNE THORPE

WAYLAND
www.waylandbooks.co.uk

First published in 2018 by Wayland
Copyright © Hodder & Stoughton, 2018

Wayland
An imprint of
Hachette Children's Group
Part of Hodder and Stoughton
Carmelite House
50 Victoria Embankment
London EC4Y 0DZ

www.hachette.co.uk

Editor: Julia Bird
Designer: RockJaw Creative

PB ISBN: 978 1 5263 0675 3

Printed in Dubai

Please note: The statistics in this book were correct at the time of printing, but because of the nature of sport, it cannot be guaranteed that they are now accurate.

The words of footballers that appear in this book are taken from press interviews and other sources.

Picture credits: Odd Andersen/AFP/Getty Images: 2l, 16r. Matthew Ashton/AMA/Getty Images: 19b. Sergei Bachlakov/Shutterstock: 4t. Robert Beck/Sports Illustrated//Getty Images: 23tl. Christian Bertrand/Shutterstock: 25tr. Frederick J. Brown/AFP/Getty Images: 2r, 17b. Chris Brunskill-FIFA/Getty Images: 19t. Jean Catuffe/Getty Images: 26. Stanley Chou/Getty Images: 29c. Robert Cianflone-FIFA/Getty Images: 13t. EFE News Agency/Alamy: 24. Keiran Galvin/NurPhoto/Getty Images: 15t. Otto Greule Jr/Getty Images: 8. Dennis GrombkowskiGetty Images: 9b. Maja Hitij/Getty Images: 20b. Catherine Ivill/AMA/Getty Images: 3, 11b, 27b. Paul Jenkins/Action Plus//Getty Images: 14t. Christof Koepsel/Getty Images: 23r. Christopher Lee-FIFA/Getty Images: 25bl. Alex Livesey/Getty Images: 28bl. Ian MacNicol/Getty Images: 27t. David Madison/Getty Images: 9t. Stephen Marques/Shutterstock: 6-7, 14-15. B. Marshall/Fox/Hulton Archive/Getty Images: 23bl. Buda Mendes/Getty Images: 18. Dean Mouhtaropoulos/Getty Images: 17t. Dan Mullan/Getty Images: front cover, 1. NurPhoto/Getty Images: 6b. Paparazzo-family/Dreamstime: 20t. Adam Pulicicchio/Getty Images: 13b. A. Ricardo/Shutterstock: 5. Graeme Shannon/Shutterstock: 28 bg. Luis Lopes Silva/Dreamstime: 22. Brad Smith/Rex/Shutterstock: 25tl. Bob Thomas/Popperfoto/Getty Images: 4b. VI-Images/Getty Images: 16c. Visionhaus/Corbis via Getty Images: 12. Friedmann Vogel/Getty Images: 29t. Hiroki Watanabe/Getty Images: 7t. Leszek Wrona/Dreamstime: 21.

Every attempt has been made to clear copyright. Should there be any inadvertent omission please apply to the publisher for rectification.

Contents

A Secret History

Women's football gets more popular every year. About 750 million people watched the 2015 Women's World Cup, and France 2019 is an even bigger show.

You might think that women's football has never been as popular as it is today – but you'd be wrong.

The first female superstars

Women's football first became popular in Britain. Back in the 1910s and 1920s, women's matches regularly attracted record crowds and raised large sums for charity. Some teams even had semi-professional star players.

▲ Japanese fans at the 2015 FIFA Women's World Cup

▼ Dick, Kerr's Ladies was one of the first women's association football teams in the world.

Banned!

In 1921, the English Football Association (FA) decided that women should not be playing football. It banned women's matches from the Association's grounds and told its referees not to officiate at them. Other football associations around the world did the same. The FA ban was only completely lifted in 1971.

Women's football is back

Since the 1970s, women's football has rocketed in popularity around the world. Today there are major leagues in North and South America, Europe and Asia–Pacific countries.

▼ Sweden take on Brazil at the 2016 Olympic Games.

TIMELINE OF WOMEN'S FOOTBALL

1881
The first proper women's football match between a team from Scotland and visitors from England

1919
A women's league is started in France

1920
First international match is held between France and England

1921
The first women's games are played in Brisbane, Australia. Women's football is banned by the English FA

1922
Australian committee decides football is inappropriate for Australian women

1932
French women's league ends

1933
First Italian women's football club is formed in Milan, but closes after nine months

1969
The English Women's Football Association is formed. Unofficial European Cup is held between Denmark, England, France and Italy

1971
English FA ends ban on women's football

1973
Denmark's Elitedivisionen Women's League is formed. Ribe win the first title

1975
Women's league re-starts in France. New Zealand Women's Soccer Association is formed

1991
First Women's World Cup is held in China (the USA win)

1995
USL-W League, a national women's soccer league, is formed in the USA

1996
Women's National Soccer League launched in Australia

Major Leagues

If you want to see the world's top female football players in action, where do you go? To one of the world's major leagues of course! This map shows you some of the biggest.

FRAUEN BUNDESLIGA

Country: **Germany**
Season: **October–May/June**
Number of teams: **12**
Biggest teams: **TSV Siegen**
Grün-Weiss Brauweiler
FFC Frankfurt

The Frauen Bundesliga features mainly home-grown players. The quality of play is high and there are some fierce rivalries between teams.

NATIONAL WOMEN'S SOCCER LEAGUE

Country: **USA**
Season: **April-October**
Number of teams: **10**
Biggest teams: **North Carolina Courage**
Portland Thorns
Orlando Pride

Formed in 2012, the NWSL is where many of the world's top female players, from Marta (see p.18) to Australian star Sam Kerr, play.

WOMEN'S SUPER LEAGUE 1

Country: **England**
Season: **November–April**
Number of teams: **10**
Biggest teams: **Chelsea**
Arsenal
Manchester City

Crowds of thousands watch popular WSL 1 matches live. Alongside the WSL is the Women's FA Cup competition, which in 2015 saw a record crowd of 30,710.

NADESHIKO LEAGUE

Country: **Japan**
Season: **March–October**
Number of teams: **10**
Biggest teams: **Nippon TV Beleza**
INAC Kobe Leonessa

One team each year is relegated from the top division of the league. The only team never to have been relegated is Nippon TV Beleza.

WOMEN'S SUPER LEAGUE

Country: **China**
Season: **September–April**
Number of teams: **8**
Biggest teams: **Dalian Quanjian**
Shanghai SVAy

In 2016, big businesses began to support Chinese WSL teams. The higher wages have attracted big-name players from Africa and Europe, such as Dalian Quanjian's Asisat Oshoala (see p.25).

W LEAGUE

Country: **Australia**
Season: **October–February**
Number of teams: **9**
Biggest teams: **Canberra United**
Melbourne City

The semi-professional W League struggles to keep its best players, who can earn higher salaries elsewhere. Australian star Sam Kerr, for example, moved from Perth Glory to Sky Blue FC in the USA.

PRO PLAYER

PROFILE

Team: **USA/Manchester City**
Position: **Midfielder**
Major honours: **2015 and 2016
    FIFA Player of the Year**

**Scorer of first-ever World
Cup final hat-trick**

**Twice Olympic gold medallist
2015 World Cup winner**

Carli Lloyd

Carli Lloyd is one of the greatest footballers the USA has ever produced. She is a big-time match winner. In the final of the 2008 Olympics Carli scored the gold-medal-winning goal against Brazil. At the next Olympics, in 2012, she scored twice in the final against Japan and again won gold. What could be better? In 2015 Carli showed us, with a hat-trick in the final of the Women's World Cup, scored in the first 16 minutes of the match.

Carli was a star for her high-school and college teams. Since becoming a senior player she has been a member of several US teams, including the Chicago Red Stars, Blue Sky FC and Houston Dash. In 2016–17 she played on loan for Manchester City.

Have you always loved soccer?
From when I first played soccer at age five, that always came first. Everywhere I went I took a soccer ball.

Who has been the biggest influence on your career?
Lots of people have helped me become a better player, but probably coach James Galanis. In 2003, he designed a program for me to be the best player in the world. He helps me with the psychological side of soccer, too: how to play well under pressure.

How did you find it being a young player coming up?
It didn't come naturally for me. I had to work at it, but I would say … my team were like my family, and [games with them] were some of my most memorable moments.

How has soccer changed you?
I've come across different people, I've had to adapt to different cultures, been all around the world … no one can teach that. It makes you a strong person.

What's your best off-field experience?
Being at the Olympics [with] other Olympic athletes, to see the village … it's truly something amazing.

And on the field?
Winning two gold medals. And winning the World Cup!

▶ Carli Lloyd scores the USA's second goal against Japan in the 2015 FIFA Women's World Cup. The USA went on to win the match 5–2.

World Dream Team

What would an international dream team of female footballers look like? If you could pick players from anywhere, maybe it would look something like this.

Of course, if you ask three football fans to come up with a dream team they usually come up with at least three different teams. And probably three different formations, too. So you probably won't agree with this selection:

1 **GOALKEEPER:** Sarah Bouhaddi, **FRANCE**

4 **DEFENDER:** Nilla Fischer, **SWEDEN**
2 **CENTRAL DEFENDER:** Wendie Renard, **FRANCE**
3 **DEFENDER:** Steph Houghton, **ENGLAND (CAPTAIN)**

5 **CENTRAL MIDFIELDER:** Lena Goessling, **GERMANY**
8 **CENTRAL MIDFIELDER:** Amandine Henry, **FRANCE**
6 **CENTRAL MIDFIELDER:** Véronica Boquete, **SPAIN**
11 **WIDE MIDFIELD/WING BACK:** Ji So-yun, **SOUTH KOREA**
7 **WIDE MIDFIELD/WING BACK:** Megan Rapinoe, **USA**

9 **FORWARD:** Sam Kerr, **AUSTRALIA**
10 **FORWARD:** Marta, **BRAZIL**

Sarah Bouhaddi scoops up the ball during a UEFA Women's 2017 match.

PRO PLAYER

PROFILE

Team: **Canada/Portland Thorns**

Position: **Forward/attacking midfielder**

Major honours: **Seven times nominated as FIFA Player of the Year**

13 times Canadian Player of the Year

Twice Olympic bronze medallist

Christine Sinclair

Christine Sinclair started playing soccer for an under-seven team when she was just four years old. She was also a good basketball and baseball player: as a girl she played in the local boys' baseball league and made the all-star team. Football came first, though; today Christine is said to be one of the best female footballers of all time.

Although she mainly plays as a forward, Christine's skill at passing and her understanding of tactics mean she can also play as an attacking midfielder. Her goalscoring is fabulous: she was the leading scorer at the 2012 Olympics. By 2018, Christine was second only to Abby Wambach in international goals scored (with 173) – but was rapidly catching her up.

▲ Christine Sinclair blasts a free kick in an exhibition match against Costa Rica.

How do you think playing soccer as a youngster affected you?

[My older brother Mike] forced me to toughen up a little bit. I went to his soccer practices and his baseball practices and … I attribute a lot of where I am today [to] those experiences.

What was it like, passing Mia Hamm's international goalscoring total?

Growing up, [Mia] was the face of women's soccer … I never thought I could reach [her] level. To pass her … was pretty special for me.

Do you enjoy being captain of the Canada team? How do you do it?

I'm a quieter type of leader. I'll do anything for my team, and I'll speak up when needed, but I tend to lead more by example.

What advice would you give players before a big, important game like a final?

Just enjoy it. You don't get too many opportunities to play in finals – so enjoy it!

How do you relax?

Believe it or not, I like to [play] golf. On a nice day, I enjoy a round of golf. I also have two young nieces, so if I happen to be in Vancouver [where they live] I'm with them.

Top Clubs

Almost all of the world's best female players play for top clubs. They don't earn as much as male players, but at a top club women can still earn a living as footballers.

OLYMPIQUE LYONNAIS FÉMININ

Country: **France**
Stadium: **Groupama OL Training Centre, Lyon**
Famous players: **Wendie Renard (France)**
Lucy Bronze (England)
Shanice van de Sanden (Netherlands)

Formed as the female section of Olympique Lyon in 2004, Olympique Lyonnais has since won the French league championship ten times and the French Cup competition seven. It has also won the UEFA Women's Champions League twice.

PORTLAND THORNS FC

Country: **USA**
Stadium: **Providence Park, Portland**
Famous players: **Meghan Klingenberg (USA)**
Christine Sinclair (Canada)
Ashleigh Sykes (Australia)

Only formed in 2012, the Thorns still won the National Women's Soccer League title in 2013. In 2017 they repeated the victory.

FFC FRANKFURT

Country: **Germany**
Stadium: **Stadium am Brentanobad, Frankfurt**
Famous players: **Sophie Schmidt (Germany)**
Ana-Maria Crnogorčević (Switzerland)
Bryane Heaberlin (USA)

Germany's most successful women's team (though their deadly rivals Turbine Potsdam would hate to hear it), with seven Bundesliga titles. The club has also won the UEFA Women's Champions League a record four times.

ARSENAL WFC

Country: **England**
Stadium: **Meadow Park, Borehamwood**
Famous players: **Jodie Taylor (England)**
Sari van Veenendaal (Netherlands)
Heather O'Reilly (USA)

Formed in 1987, the Gunners are one of Europe's top teams. They have won the UEFA Women's Cup once, the WSL title twice and the FA Cup three times.

DALIAN QUANJIAN

Country: **China**
Stadium: **Jinzhou Stadium, Dalian**
Famous players: **Li Dongna (China)**
Asisat Lamina Oshoala (Nigeria)
Gaëlle Enganamouit (Cameroon)

The club was founded in 1984, and ten years later won the Chinese championship for the first time. It won the title again in 2008, 2012, 2013, 2016 and 2017.

NIPPON TV BELEZA

Country: **Japan**
Stadium: **Inagi Central Park, Tokyo Prefecture**
Famous players: **Azusa Iwashimizu (Japan)**
Mina Tanaka (Japan)

The club's name, Beleza, is Portuguese for 'beauty'. By 2017 the club had won the Division 1 championship an amazing 15 times.

Famous Goals

Fizzing long-distance shots, spectacular swerves past defenders, red-hot volleys, crunching headers – women's football has them all. Here are just a few goals from the highlights reel of international football:

ABBY WAMBACH

Position: **Forward**
Country/club: **USA/Western New York Flash**
Match: **USA v Brazil**
Where: **Dresden, Germany**
Competition: **Women's World Cup 2011**

This was Abby Wambach's most famous goal. A powerful header, scored in the 122nd minute of extra time, it meant the match was decided by penalties – which the USA won 5-3. In 2015 the goal was voted the greatest in the history of the Women's World Cup.

BEST WORLD CUP GOAL!

SUPER-COOL FINISH!

VIVIANNE MIEDEMA

Position: **Forward**
Country/club: **The Netherlands/Arsenal**
Match: **Netherlands v Sweden**
Where: **Doetinchem, The Netherlands**
Competition: **2017 European Championship**

A lightning-fast goal that has everything: scorching pace plus pin-point ball control and passing by Shanice van de Sanden in the buildup, then a cool finish by Miedema. The Netherlands went on to beat England 3-0 in the semi-final, then won the final 4-2 against Denmark.

HAT-TRICK HEROE!

Position: **Forward**
Country/club: **England/Seattle Reign**
Match: **England v Scotland**
Where: **Utrecht, The Netherlands**
Competition: **2017 European Championship**

Scotland got a 6-0 thumping in this match, with half of England's goals coming from Taylor. Her hat-trick was completed with a simple-looking goal that was actually very skillful: a brilliantly timed run, followed by a first-touch lob over the goalkeeper.

GREATEST OF ALL TIME!

MARTA

Position: **Forward**
Country/club: **Brazil/Orlando Pride**
Match: **Brazil vs USA**
Where: **Hangzhou, China**
Competition: **Women's World Cup 2007**

Marta gets the ball with her back to goal, then flicks it over her shoulder and round the defender with her left foot. She sprints past the defender on the opposite side, collects the ball and runs into the area. Marta then cuts inside another defender and slides the ball into the tiny gap between goalkeeper and post. Phew!

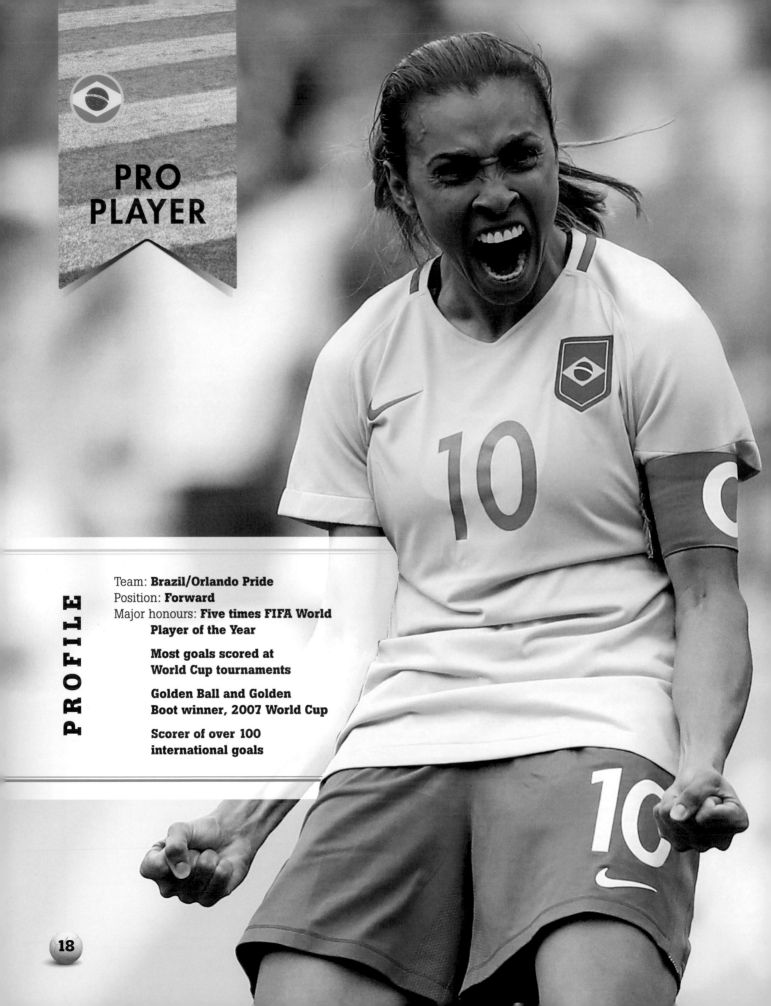

PROFILE

Team: **Brazil/Orlando Pride**
Position: **Forward**
Major honours: **Five times FIFA World Player of the Year**

Most goals scored at World Cup tournaments

Golden Ball and Golden Boot winner, 2007 World Cup

Scorer of over 100 international goals

Marta

Is Marta – whose full name is Marta Vieira da Silva – the best female footballer ever? Plenty of people think so. Marta left home at 14 to follow a career in football. By the time she was 31 she had already been voted World Player of the Year five times, and scored a long list of breathtaking goals. No defender in the world wants to see Marta running at them with the ball: her dribbling skills are legendary. Former Canadian international Martina Franko said:

"I've never played anybody as fast as her. I've never seen anyone who runs as fast as you, then as soon as she touches the ball, gets faster."

Marta's shooting and dead-ball skills are just as good.

What got you into football?
My story isn't that different from the stories of many other girls. We always begin playing for fun, playing with friends on the street, in any space we can find close to home ... I began this way too, playing with my cousins.

When did you first realise you were a good player?
I have always played with boys since the beginning, and sometimes with boys who were a little older than me – and I noticed that I was always standing out ... I noticed I was pretty good.

How has football changed since you started your career?
People [back then] did not look kindly upon a girl playing football with a load of boys, and my family thought in the same way. I think today people really watch [the women's game], they like the women's national team, people support it in Brazil ... so it's become popular.

What advice would you give young players today?
It's still difficult today, but it's a bit easier than it was when I started out. So you have to seize the moment, chase your dreams and believe in yourself.

▲ Marta speeds past two Japanese players during the 2017 Tournament of Nations.

International competitions

For most fans, the best chance of seeing the world's top women footballers on TV (or even live, if you're lucky) is at a big competition.

▲ Fans of the China women's team, heading for the 2019 World Cup and dreaming of a first ever win.

▼ The final of the 2017 Euros: Sherida Spitse of the Netherlands drills a free kick at the Denmark goal.

The World Cup

The biggest competition of all is the FIFA World Cup. Every team except the hosts has to play in qualifying leagues to win one of the 24 places.

At the World Cup itself, the teams are split into six groups of four. Each team in a group plays the others; the two with the best results qualify for the knockout stages. The four best third-place teams also get into the knockout stages, making 16 teams in total. After that if you lose, you go home.

Other big competitions

After the World Cup, the next-biggest tournament in women's football is the Olympics. There are also big regional competitions, including the European Championship (Euros), South America's Copa América, North America's CONCACAF Championship, the Asian Cup, and the Africa Women's Cup of Nations.

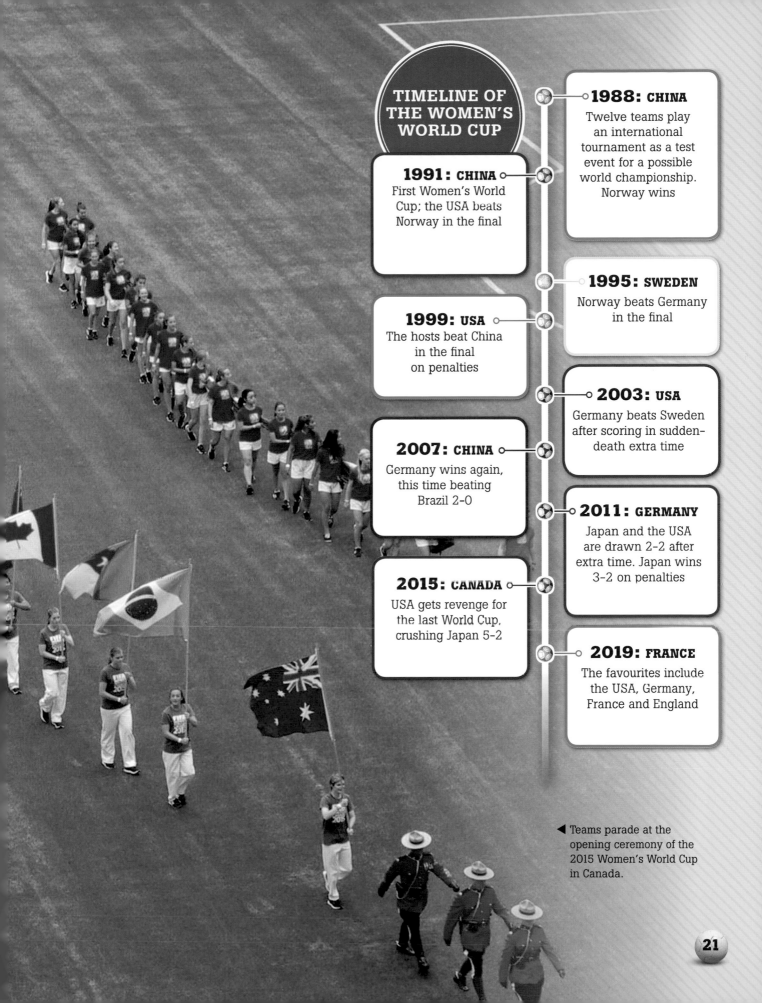

TIMELINE OF THE WOMEN'S WORLD CUP

1988: CHINA
Twelve teams play an international tournament as a test event for a possible world championship. Norway wins

1991: CHINA
First Women's World Cup; the USA beats Norway in the final

1995: SWEDEN
Norway beats Germany in the final

1999: USA
The hosts beat China in the final on penalties

2003: USA
Germany beats Sweden after scoring in sudden-death extra time

2007: CHINA
Germany wins again, this time beating Brazil 2-0

2011: GERMANY
Japan and the USA are drawn 2-2 after extra time. Japan wins 3-2 on penalties

2015: CANADA
USA gets revenge for the last World Cup, crushing Japan 5-2

2019: FRANCE
The favourites include the USA, Germany, France and England

◀ Teams parade at the opening ceremony of the 2015 Women's World Cup in Canada.

Record breakers

Until recently, a female who wanted to play football had to be pretty determined (and in some countries they still do). Perhaps that's why the record books are filled with some amazing achievements.

PLAYERS WITH 150+ INTERNATIONAL GOALS

In 2017 the list looked like this:

1	Abby Wambach (now retired)	**USA**	**184 goals**
2	Christine Sinclair	**Canada**	**169 goals**
3	Mia Hamm (now retired)	**USA**	**158 goals**

TOP GOALKEEPER

Hope Solo was the USA's number one goalkeeper from 2005–2016. She was the first international goalkeeper ever to reach 100 shutout matches (when she did not let in a single goal). Her teams won over 150 international games, and Solo won over 200 caps.

▶ Hope Solo, whose international goalkeeping record is unmatched in women's or men's football.

TOP GOALIE!

HIGHEST-PAID PLAYER

Female players are nothing like as well paid as male ones. The best-paid female footballer in 2016 was said to be Marta, at US$500,000 a year, or nearly US$42,000 a month. Compare that to Portugal's Cristiano Ronaldo, who apparently earned almost US$2 million a month!

BIGGEST CROWD

A crowd of 90,185 watched USA beat China in the 1999 World Cup final. It was not only the biggest crowd ever at a women's football match, but also a world record for any women's sports event.

▼ The USA team celebrate wildly after winning the 1999 World Cup final.

BIGGEST CROWD!

INTERNATIONAL AGE EXTREMES

Oldest: Lily Parr of England was the oldest international player. She was 46 years and 89 days old when she played against France in 1951. She scored to become the oldest international goalscorer, too.

Youngest: Alyssa Chin was just 13 years and 17 days old when she appeared for the Cayman Islands against Puerto Rico. The youngest goalscorer is Alina Litvinenko of Ukraine, who was 13 years and 131 days old when she scored against Palestine. One of the youngest international hat-tricks must have been Pernille Harder's. The Denmark striker scored three times against Georgia when she was only 16.

◄ Lily Parr, one of the first and greatest female players, performs an early version of the Usain Bolt 'lightning' pose.

► Pernille Harder, who exploded onto the international football scene when she was just 16 years old.

OLDEST PLAYER!

TEENAGE HAT-TRICK!

Stars of the future

Great new female players are appearing on the scene all the time – so which young players are the ones to watch out for at the 2019 World Cup and beyond?

DEYNA CASTELLANOS

Country: **Venezuela**
Position: **Forward**
Team: **Florida State Seminoles**

Power and pace, plus excellent ball-control skills, make this young Venezuelan player one of the hottest prospects in the women's game.

FAST **FORWARD!**

ASHLEY SANCHEZ

Country: **USA**
Position: **Forward**
Team: **UCLA Bruins**

Sanchez is the only US player to play in two World Cups in a single year (2016), when she was part of the under-17 and under-20 World Cups. A good bet as a future senior team star.

KADEISHA BUCHANAN

Country: **Canada**
Position: **Defender**
Team: **Olympique Lyonnais**

For a 19-year-old defender to be nominated as Best Young Player at the 2015 World Cup, they have to be special. To actually win, as Buchanan did, shows that they are a star of the future.

CHINESE STAR!

ASISAT OSHOALA

Country: **Nigeria**
Position: **Forward/attacking midfielder**
Team: **Dalian Quanjian**

Oshoala's decision to drop out of school to be a footballer has paid off. Having played for Liverpool and Arsenal in the UK, she moved to Chinese club Dalian for a salary reported to be around six times as high.

LIEKE MARTENS

Country: **Netherlands**
Position: **Attacking midfielder/forward**
Team: **Barcelona**

Martens is not a new face, having been a member of the Netherlands national team since 2011. In 2017, though, her playing was so outstanding that she won the FIFA Best Women's Player award.

WORLD'S BEST!

YOUNG CAPTAIN!

GEORGIA STANWAY

Country: **England**
Position: **Forward**
Team: **Manchester City**

The young striker (left) was just 16 and still at school when she made her senior début for Manchester City in 2015. In 2016 she captained England's under-17s to a bronze medal at the European Championship, as well as scoring the WSL-1 Goal of the Season.

Refereeing and managing

The number of female coaches and referees is growing all the time. This means players now have a way to stay in the game when their playing career is over.

Officials

Attitudes to female officials have changed a lot. In 2006, Luton Town manager Mike Newell criticised the appearance of a woman, Amy Rayner, as assistant referee:

"She shouldn't be here… This is not park football, so what are women doing here?"

Even then, Newell sounded foolish: female officials had been taking charge of important games for a long time. Years before, at the third Women's World Cup in 1999, the pool of referees had been all-female for the first time in history.

Coaches and managers

In top leagues coaches and managers were once all male, but this is changing. In Europe, for example, the number of female coaches with a UEFA Pro Licence (the highest level) went from 64 in 2015 to 101 in 2016.

▼ Corinne Diacre, the first female manager to coach a top-flight men's team. Diacre has since left Clermont Ferrand to coach the French women's side.

The referee speaks

Sian Massey-Ellis MBE is a groundbreaking female official. She became a professional referee in 2010, and was the first female official to work in England's Premier League.

How did you become a professional referee?
I started refereeing youth football, and [moved] through the ranks through semi-professional to professional football. You go step by step.

Did you enjoy refereeing youth football?
I used to love it!

Do you see yourself as a bit of a role model?
I'd like to think so … if I inspire one or two girls to [become an official] I've done a good job.

What's your favourite match as a referee?
[Sian can't pick one, so she picks three] My first professional match … my first Premiership match … and the women's Euros.

◄ Assistant referee Sian Massey-Ellis runs the line during a fast-flowing Premier League match between Crystal Palace and Chelsea football teams.

Five fun football facts

Women's football is not just about World Cups and earning Player of the Year awards. Most players never get to such a high level – but that doesn't mean there's nothing interesting about them …

Mum's the word

When 17-year-old Karen Carney scored the winning goal for England against Finland in the 2005 UEFA Women's Championship in stoppage time, she was super excited. Unfortunately, Karen's mum noticed that her celebrations included some bad language – and gave Karen a good telling off as a result!

The highest match

In 2017, the highest-ever football match took place on Mount Kilimanjaro in Tanzania. A group of female footballers from 20 different countries played 90 minutes of 11-a-side football at 5,790 metres altitude. Ten years earlier FIFA had officially banned games being played above 2,500 metres because they were too tough – so it was no surprise that the players took it easy and the game ended 0-0.

▼ Karen Carney shouts in delight after scoring a dramatic last-gasp winner against Finland.

▲ Watch out for altitude sickness! The highest-ever football match was played on the snowy summit of Mount Kilimanjaro.

The (Brazilian) Equatorial Guinea team

Equatorial Guinea really wanted to do well at the 2016 Olympics. In fact, they wanted to do so well that they decided to select almost a whole team of Brazilian players – 10 of them. As a result Equatorial Guinea was banned from the 2020 Olympics and the 2019 World Cup.

▶ Laetitia Chapeh Yimga, Dorine Nina Chuigoue and Diala Blessing of Equatorial Guinea, three members of the Equatorial Guinea team that turned out to be mostly from Brazil.

▲ The North Korean women's football team were banned from the 2019 FIFA World Cup.

Eighth-ranked losers

Football is a serious business in North Korea, and leading up to the 2015 World Cup North Korea was ranked number 8 in the world. Then it was discovered some players had used performance-enhancing drugs at the previous World Cup: the entire team was banned as a result.

Riot girls

The first big women's football match we know about happened in Edinburgh in May 1881. Despite playing in knickerbockers and high-heeled boots, the Scottish team beat England 3-0. At the rematch a few days later, a crowd invaded the pitch and started a riot. The game had to be called off.

FIFA Women's World Cup Winners

YEAR	VENUE	WINNER	SECOND	THIRD
1991	China	USA	Norway	Sweden
1995	Sweden	Norway	Germany	USA
1999	USA	USA	China	Brazil
2003	USA	Germany	Sweden	USA
2007	China	Germany	Brazil	USA
2011	Germany	Japan	USA	Sweden
2015	Canada	USA	Japan	England
2019	France	–	–	–

FIFA Women Footballers of the Year

YEAR	WINNER		YEAR	WINNER	
2001	Mia Hamm	USA	2010	Marta	BRAZIL
2002	Mia Hamm	USA	2011	Homare Sawa	JAPAN
2003	Birgit Prinz	GERMANY	2012	Abby Wambach	USA
2004	Birgit Prinz	GERMANY	2013	Nadine Angerer	GERMANY
2005	Birgit Prinz	GERMANY	2014	Nadine Kessler	GERMANY
2006	Marta	BRAZIL	2015	Carli Lloyd	USA
2007	Marta	BRAZIL	2016	Carli Lloyd	USA
2008	Marta	BRAZIL	2017	Lieke Martens	NETHERLANDS
2009	Marta	BRAZIL	2018	Marta	BRAZIL

Glossary

altitude height above sea level. As the height increases, the amount of oxygen in the air decreases, making it harder for athletes to work hard.

cap award for playing for your country; for example a player with three caps has played for their country three times.

CONCACAF Confederation of North, Central American and Caribbean Association Football.

dead ball ball that has been placed down and is not moving (so, a free kick, penalty kick or corner).

extra time Time added on to a match if the game is a draw after the normal 90 minutes.

FIFA Fédération Internationale de Football Association, the international governing body of football, which organises the World Cup.

Golden Ball award for the player judged to be the best at the World Cup.

Golden Boot award for the player who scores most goals at the World Cup.

hat-trick three goals scored by the same player in one game.

knickerbockers baggy trousers that come to below the knee and are usually worn tucked into long socks. Stylish!

lob kick that goes high into the air and drops down steeply.

MBE Member of the British Empire, an award given to leading citizens.

officiate act as an official, such as a referee or assistant referee.

on loan when a player for one club goes to play for another temporarily

outfield non-goalkeeping.

pool group or gathering.

psychological to do with how a person is thinking and feeling.

semi-professional paid, but not full time.

shutout game in which the opposition does not score a goal.

stoppage time time added to the end of the match to account for stoppages (such as play being stopped because a player is injured).

sudden-death form of extra time where the first team to score wins the match.

Index